STRENGTHEN YOUR PERFORMANCE
IN PSYCHOLOGICAL TESTS

Strengthen Your Performance in Psychological Tests

Cécile Césari

foulsham
LONDON · NEW YORK · TORONTO · SYDNEY

foulsham

The Publishing House, Bennetts Close,
Cippenham, Berkshire, SL1 5AP, England

ISBN 0-572-0228-5

Copyright original French edition © 1989 Marabout, Alleur (Belgique)
Copyright this English language edition © 1996 W. Foulsham & Co. Ltd

Typeset by Poole Typesetting (Wessex) Ltd
Translated by Julian Worthington
Printed in Great Britain by
St. Edmundsbury Press, Bury St. Edmunds

Contents

Introduction

Anyone may at some time find themselves having to under-go professional selection by sitting a test. The aim of this book is to explain what this type of selection consists of and how best a candidate can prepare for it.

A large part of the book is devoted to examples and exercises of tests most commonly used on people applying for jobs so that you can familiarise yourself with what is involved and not be anxious about tackling this type of exam.

With this in mind, the book has been specially prepared as a guide for candidates, covering a range of different tests which those applying for jobs are likely to have to resolve. Each test comes with a short commentary and, of course, answers.

The different characteristics of the various selection tests have been covered in relation to their construction as much as to their use. Certain technical aspects, such as scaling and assessment, have been ignored here since they will be of little value to the reader and only really concern the expert examiners.

Part 1

Methods of Assessment

Methods of Assessment

Definition

A test consists of a precise questionnaire, identical for all candidates being examined, which incorporates specific techniques for evaluating success or failure based on a points system.

Every test includes a standardised situation with a definite task to complete – the same for all those participating. Each result is gauged by statistical comparison with that of the other candidates under the same conditions. This enables the examiner to classify each candidate with reference to the average success of the whole group or, by means of typological characteristics, to place individuals within a certain group.

From the results obtained through these tests, an overall mark can be awarded in comparison with those obtained by a reference group and enable each candidate to be classified within a particular range.

These general conditions can be applied to all tests, particularly those aimed at assessing intelligence, aptitude or individual aspects about a person – for example, one's character.

So the object of this type of test is to evaluate the capacity of individuals in comparison to others by means of a scale or to measure the individual differences through a system developed from the answers given by the group as a whole. For example, if a candidate has 20, 30 or 40 right answers, then points are awarded on that basis (1,2 or 3) which will enable his or her score to be set against the average obtained by the reference group and thus a comparison made.

Such results should enable the examiner to predict the potential success or future of each candidate in a specific career or position.

The standardisation of the test situation, accurate recording of results and strict application of a scale system are all indispensable and fundamental conditions for the correct application of any test of this kind.

Advice for the candidate

Before describing the principle tests use by selection agencies, it is important to underline that those sitting a test – whether it is to measure intelligence, aptitude or reasoning – can be influenced by factors that have nothing to do with intelligence, logical aptitude or general reasoning.

The degree of a candidate's motivation, the interest he shows in the test, the physical or mental state he is in with regard to the nature of the exercises can be a decisive influence on the final results.

As far as the personality tests are concerned, each individual will tend to orientate his answers in such a way as to display himself in the best possible light. But one should also bear in mind that the personality of the examiner can intervene in the interpretation of such answers.

It is clear that these and other elements do put into perspective the final assessment of the candidate

In order to avoid some elementary mistakes, it is important to prepare oneself for this kind of test. Here are just a few examples of what to do – and what not to do.

· **Preparing oneself for a test by trying to memorise all the right answers offers no guarantee of success.**
A series of excellent scores against established average statistics may well raise suspicion and an examiner might find such results slightly curious. Such a reaction could easily work against the candidate.

· **The profile requested often varies according to the job**

and, in the case of an identical job, according to the company involved.
It is important to make a separate analysis of the nature of each job concerned and the demands that go with it.

· **Companies, associations or institutions looking for personnel may not only be recruiting for exceptional individuals but, quite simply, someone suitable for a particular position.**
In such a case, trying to achieve the top score is clearly not the best strategy.

The established phrase 'good probability of success' simply means that the candidate will have to display a certain number of necessary characteristics in order to carry out the work required. So the set of tests used will serve to take stock of the qualities required for success in any given job and assume the examination of a minimum level of capability. The conditions asked for can, as has already been said, vary according to the vacancy in question.

So it is up to the candidate (as well as the company) to define precisely the required profile. There are always several.

The ideal course for a would-be candidate, before sitting any test, is to make his own analysis of the work required in respect of the position for which he is applying. He must first of all be clear about what exactly is be asked for in order to determine as best he can what qualities and skills will be necessary for a successful application – capability, knowledge, motivation, personality, etc – and the level that must be achieved in each.

The criteria can be very different. Are, for example, manual skills required? Is it a question of being able to complete a task quickly and accurately? Or does one need to be able to communicate, for example where one is in regular contact with the public, to take the initiative or to assume responsibility?

One must first evaluate such requirements and weigh up their relative importance: intelligence and the ability to reason, taking orders or handling human relations are all difficult areas to define and, equally, demonstrate.

The point has already been made – and this is the other

important aspect – **that the company's objectives must also be taken into consideration.** This could amount to increasing, diversifying or rationalising production, improving working relationships, imposing restrictions or effecting economies. Close attention must be paid to any specific or peculiar aspect of the job required.

To recap, analysis of the work to be carried out and careful observation both of others holding the same position and also the company's aims and principal techniques are three essential elements in preparing for any test.
Such information on the general conditions surrounding the vacancy must give any candidate more confidence to tackle the kind of questions he will have to answer. For each job profile a certain number of qualities and skills will be examined, according to various criteria.

Test strategy

The best possible strategy is, above all, to reply simply and clearly to the questions being asked and to avoid, if possible, deviating from the given format.
As far as how to obtain the right results is concerned, there is no single answer here. Two people receiving the same marks can have achieved them through different means. It is possible, for example, to pay careful attention to the first part of a question and to ignore the second, to sacrifice accuracy for speed or to reply to those questions that are more easy or straightforward and return later to fill in the gaps.
So it is not possible to elaborate on individual strategies by way of establishing principles. But one should always bear in mind that certain tests penalise incorrect answers, while others judge the absence of an answer as a wrong one. So there can be pitfalls for those who decide to leave gaps for some of the questions. For example, the examiner may take this as an indication of lack of knowledge and deduct points accordingly. Being consistent in one's replies can prove an asset in terms of general approach and technique.

Other selection criteria

Apart from intelligence tests, there are other ways in which potential employers can differentiate between candidates, the most important of which include:

- Relevant diplomas and certificates
- Professional experience (including testimonials from previous employers)
- Professional achievements
- Career statistics
- CV analysis
- Medical check
- Interview with a psychologist.

On the whole, intelligence tests provide a limited perspective of the candidates, which should reassure all those who have to sit them. The information they provide must be supplemented by other procedures and considered in conjunction with the details contained in the applicant's file. They cannot on their own be regarded as a guarantee of satisfactory or successful selection.

Instructions and marking

With every test there will be some explanatory notes, including the physical conditions, amount of time allowed, the situation chosen as a standard and what this is, as well as general instructions.

During the examination, the psychologist in charge of the test will give instructions to the candidates and explain to them what they have to do and the time they have available. These instructions are also contained in the test papers that each will receive.

The use of different methods for marking the answers helps to insure the fairest interpretation of the results and each individual's eventual classification. This amounts to adding up the points for all the correct answers and equally deducting points for incorrect answers in order to obtain an overall mark.

With the final marks achieved, each of the examined candidates can be classified and it is through this procedure that a selection is made from the group of applicants.

Part 2

Evaluation and Personality Tests

Evaluation and Personality Tests

The principal tests

There are basically two categories of tests that you will come across – either published in books such as this one or employed by recruitment agencies. In the case of the latter, the tests are more specific since they are generally adapted to suit individual clients and their particular businesses.

The standard tests most commonly used are:

- **D48, Matrix 47 and R85:** ability to reason logically and mathematically.
- **BV16, VB17 and D70 (vocabulary test):** verbal intelligence and expression.
- **GZ, 16PF, Rozensweig's Frustration Test, Rorschach and MMPI:** personality and project tests.

Within these tests, which are frequently used, it is important to distinguish between those that involve one's efficiency (related to skill, capability and knowledge) and those concerned with one's personality, which look to measure particular aspects of the individual – sociability, emotion, character and behaviour.

The difference between the two is quite distinct. One involves intelligence in its most general sense, for which different types of test are used. The other is based purely on personality.

Efficiency tests

Intelligence tests for adults use specific material: for example the Wechsler-Bellevue intelligence scale which covers eleven categories. There are comprehension tests (involving different questions on general knowledge) and information tests (which include questions on practical knowledge such as "What does one need to be able to travel in Europe?") and tests on similarities (which consist, for example, of grouping figures, images and objects in relation to their common characteristics), instant memory and simple arithmetic.

Other types of test also exist for measuring one's intellectual functions: for example, reasoning skills which can be more accurately analysed through exercises that involve deduction and inference. This is the case with D48 or the dominoes test, which gets progressively more difficult. It assumes a time limit of 25 seconds for each puzzle (or question) and involves a wide variety of geometric symbols.

This type of test distinguishes between ability and application and is able to measure one's skill in changing from one type of reasoning to another. The information and its general structure change with each item. Such exercises can be compared with those of Matrix 47, BV53 or MGM.

The reasoning test, which is very often used by recruitment agencies, is made up of 40 questions of different formats: palindromes, series of numbers and letters and reconstitution of words, for example. The time allowed is 20 minutes.

Here is an example of the type of exercise included in this test:

XXX 6 – VII 4 – XVIII 7 – XIII ?

With each Roman numeral there is a corresponding Arabic number, save the last. You need to find the missing one to complete the series. To solve this exercise, you need to spot that the number of strokes making up each Roman numeral is equivalent to the Arabic number: XXX has 6 strokes, VII has 4, XVIII has 7 and therefore the missing number for XIII is 5.

Other methods can be used to reach the right answer, but we are not going to detail them here.

Tests designed to determine verbal comprehension are equally numerous and regularly used: BV8, BV50 and BV51, BV16/17 and D70, thoughts, proverbs, series of words in relation to an idea or type of reasoning. With each series of five or six words there is a common subject or theme. It is necessary to eliminate those words that do not correspond or match with this – the 'odd ones out'.

There are equally other types of exercise used in vocabulary tests. Here is an example:

c etal – c lian – c late – c ?

The word 'etal' is 'late' backwards. Therefore the answer is 'nail' – i.e. 'lian' backwards.

Personality tests

Project and personality tests form an assessment group distinct from the efficiency, aptitude or intelligence tests, which use a numerical system of evaluation. The value of the latter system is that it is statistical, its measure metric and the scale fixed: so the score achieved is definitive. The function of an aptitude or intelligence test is objective.

The project and personality tests reveal one or more tendencies or characteristics which a psychologist can pick up and interpret according to its subjectivity and in the general context of the job concerned. Bearing in mind the diversity of what can be measured, the general basis of such tests is therefore very vague.

There are all sorts of tests that will look to earmark one's individuality through different means. While one will reveal certain personal characteristics in the context of work, others will seek to determine certain relational qualities, such as the influence on others, flexibility or adaptability.

This group of tests, which includes that of Guilford-Zimmerman, does not search for information that covers what it is understood by personality such as one gleans from tests like Rorschach (ink-stain test) or TAT. The latter have an essentially clinical bias which looks into personality in the pathological sense of the word.

The make-up and objective of project tests are close to those of clinical questionnaires administered by doctors, which are kept confidential but used in the medical field (questions about anxiety, stress or autism) and which only concern very obliquely the professional world.

It is therefore necessary to distinguish between personality (in the clinical sense) and personal characteristics, notably those which are able to influence one's behaviour at work.

By way of an example, we will mention some attempts at investigating personality which were carried out using the Rorschach method, comparing them with tests like the temperament assessment of Guilford-Zimmerman, Kuder's professional preference test or Cattel's 16PF.

Project tests: Rorschach

The Rorschach test is made up of 10 bicoloured rectangular boards representing ink stains obtained by folding paper. The candidates must interpret the shapes and explain in a few words what they represent for them.

Each reply is precisely noted by the psychologist who also registers any reactions, hesitations or emotions aroused by the presentation of the boards. One's interpretation can focus on the detail or the whole image, its shape, colour, content and so on.

We should say straight away that Rorschach sees in any interpretation of the white background the sign of an opposing attitude, the desire to contradict, to contravene or attack, where average candidates would be inclined to interpret the stain.

A large number of replies based on the white background can indicate a schizoid personality with a spirit of opposition and difficulty in adapting, even the obstacles and negative attitudes associated with schizophrenia, hypochondria or depression.

On the other hand, more than 50 per cent of replies which involve animal shapes indicates stereotype or automatic thought on a psychotic subject, especially when these answers concentrate on minute detail (only 30 per cent of such answers are given by the average candidate). On the other hand, less than 30 per cent can indicate a destruction of the mental processes.

Finally, we should say that replies regarded as 'commonplace' are registered by a third of candidates, who have a tendency to see such stains as representing a butterfly, a bat, men waving, people's heads, a team of dancers, etc. Such answers are regarded as an expression of sociability and indicate the degree of participation and adaptability on the part of the candidate to the idea of collectivity and professional life.

To summarise, only replies 'G' and 'D' can be considered definitively as of the 'right form'. Essentially they relate to the distinction between the whole (the global form) or the part (the detail). The G form is taken in its entirety and understood to have the property of synthesis, theoretic intelligence and the conceptual capacity for the subject. In contrast, the D form only contains a part of the stain and indicates practical intelligence and a good adaptation to the subject in daily life.

Personality tests: factor analysis

Personality tests, such as the temperament assessment of Guilford-Zimmerman, Kuder, MBTI (Myers-Bridge) or Cattell's 16PF, search for quite another kind of information, as we shall see.

These tests are not looking to reveal the pathological or supposed personality of candidates, but rather those personal characteristics relating to their ability to adapt to the world around them and to their social and professional life.

What is going to be revealed and analysed by the specialists concerns the personal traits defined by factor analysis, which will be interpreted in conjunction with a profile corresponding to a predetermined job or profession: combativeness, subtlety or understanding in situations of conflict; the degree of sociability or the importance given to the action; tolerance to frustration, stress, criticism, etc.

With the analysis, the experts are equally going to look to determine certain tendencies such as introversion or extroversion, the predominance of judgement or perception and the candidate's main areas of interest, all of which constitute specific methods of approach in establishing the reality and, within reason, the social or professional conduct of each individual.

This type of test, which appears with questions on social attitudes and includes each time between nine and sixteen factors, aims equally at stirring up individual reactions to subjects as diverse as publicity, fashion or male-female relationships: for example, the conservative-liberal axis analysed by the 16PF test which measures sixteen personality factors.

The distinction between project and personality tests is therefore important. But this project dimension has not been included in the practical examples that follow. We have tried, on the contrary, to give as much space as possible to those types of test currently adapted to the world of work and one's social life, similar to those that the reader can expect to face in the various selection procedures he or she may have to undergo.

Part 3

Practical Tests

Practical Tests

1. Efficiency tests

SERIES OF NUMBERS AND LETTERS

1. Write the missing numbers in place of the question marks:

   a 96/94 – 98/102 – 106/104 – 108/112 – ?
   b 19 – 1 – 220 – 4 – 190 – 1 – 240 – 6 – 77 – ?
   c 2 – 6 – 8 – 2 – 4 – 6 – 2 – 4 – ? – 3 – 9 –
   12 – 3 – 4 – ?
   d 12 – 6 – 17 – 14 – 16 – 29 – 128 – 140 –
   267 – 19 – 2 – ?

2. Write the two missing numbers under the last word:

ICICLE	HELICOPTER	POPULATION	PLANE	READ
3+3	4+6	5+5	2+3	?

3. Write the missing number under the last word:

WAITING	ARRIVAL	ENORMOUS	ALPHABETICAL	POOR
1	2	0	3	?

Answers

1a. 116/114
Note that the first number of each pair of numbers is sepa-

rated from the previous (i.e. the second number of the pair before it) by a value equal to + 4:

96/94   98/102   106/104   108/112   **116/...**
  + 4   + 4   + 4   +4

Now look at the second number in each pair, which changes regularly and alternately by a value equal to – 2 and then + 4. So the second of the missing numbers is **116 – 2 = 114.**

1b. 5
Note that each single-digit number is the result of the sum of the digits of the previous number which carries three:

19 : 1 + 9 = 10 : 1 + 0 = 1   –   220 : 2 + 2 + 0 = 4   etc

With the last number in the sequence being 77, the calculation is as follows: 7 + 7 = 14: 1 + 4 = 5.

1c. 6 and 7
Note the regular succession of three numbers, the third being the sum of the previous two.

1d. 20
Here again note a succession of three numbers, the third being the sum of the previous two minus one.

2. READ – 2 + 2
In this puzzle, the two numbers under each word correspond to the number of vowels and consonants respectively in each word.

3. POOR – 0
Here the number under each word corresponds to the number of As in each word. In the case of the word POOR, there are no As. Hence the answer is 0.

COMMON SENSE

1. Indicate with a cross, from the replies suggested for the following question, the two that appear the most applicable:

    To make an omelette one must:
    a. Light the gas under the pan.
    b. Break open the eggs.

c. Be hungry.
d. Use a frying pan.
e. Know how to make an omelette.

2. In the following sentence, underline the words that seem to you incomprehensible:

The countess left at five o'clock and got down from her tree; it was cold.

Answers

1. Two sets of answers are possible here:

   b. Break open the eggs AND
   d. Use a frying pan
   OR
   c. Be hungry AND
   e. Know how to make an omelette.

2. **And got down from her tree** is incomprehensible.

VERBAL LOGIC

1. Underline in each of the following series the three words corresponding to the one proposed:

   Example: HAND
   flower – <u>thumb</u> – manual – ring – <u>nail</u> – <u>finger</u>

   a. FOOD
   lotion – cat – roast – paw – loaf – vegetable

   b. HOUSE
   woodwork – heating – smoked – roof – children – walls

2. Underline in the following series the three words nearest to the one proposed:

   a. FEATHER
   bird – light – plumage – fly – wind – write

   b. NEWSPAPER
   paper – ink – news – journalist – headline – information

3. Underline the three words that do not belong in the following series:

   late – bend – return – spend – look – regard

4. Choose from the following synonyms the three which seem to define best the word MEASURE:

   estimate – calculate – evaluate – appreciate – survey – judge – meter

5. Underline the three words you think would be synonyms for AVAILABLE:

   receptive – willing – vacant – open – free – unoccupied – organised

6. Find another word that sounds the same as each of the following:

   Examples: pour = poor
   there = their

   bare – flew – floor – here – liar
   loan – peace – peer – saw – spade
   taught – tear – towed – wail – whether

7. Decode the following sentence in which certain letters have been replaced by symbols:

   ¤he #e§ ~s ~n m§ poc#e¤
   ¤ = ?   # = ?   § = ?   ~ = ?

8. Find the sentence contained in each of the two following lines (two solutions are possible):

   * Whetiremetheandre'stiadewiwallittheforre'snoamanway
   * Theroearmelywasbin'trdbucatiltchesintheawodayrm

9. Explain in one line to what, according to you, the following words correspond and what you think they have in common:

   Example: polish – rag – brush
   These three objects are all used for cleaning shoes.

a. Colchester – Brighton – Hounslow
b. campaign – exercise – operation
c. earthquake – hurricane – avalanche
d. Winston – Charles – Adolf
e. Luke – John – Matthew
f. arch – soffit – rib
g. epoch – era – season
h. tripod – trio – triple
i. trunk – bark – branch
j. swing – cantilever – suspension
k. acute – grave – circumflex
l. butler – maid – valet

Answers

1a. FOOD: **roast – loaf – vegetable**
1b. HOUSE: **woodwork – roof – walls**

2a. FEATHER: **bird – plumage – fly**
2b. NEWSPAPER: **news – headline – information**

3. <u>late</u> – <u>return</u> – <u>look</u>
These three words were underlined as not belonging to the series. The other words had a common factor – they all ended with the letter **d**.

4. <u>calculate</u> – <u>survey</u> – <u>meter</u>

5. <u>vacant</u> – <u>free</u> – <u>unoccupied</u>

6. bear – 'flu – flaw – hear – lyre
lone – piece – pier – sore – spayed
taut – tier – toad – whale – weather

7. The key is in my pocket
$\square$ = t   # = k   § = y   ~ = i

8. Where there's a will there's a way or
Time and tide wait for no man
*Whe/ti/re/me/the/and/re's/ti/a/de/wi/wa/ll/it/the/
for/re's/no/a/man/way
and
The early bird catches the worm or

Rome wasn't built in a day
*The/ro/ear/me/ly/was/bi/n't/rd/bu/cat/ilt/ches/
in/the/a/wo/day/rm

9. **a.** All the towns are in counties ending with 'sex' –
   Essex, Sussex and Middlesex.
   b. All three words have a military context.
   c. All three words relate to natural catastrophes.
   d. Winston Churchill, Charles de Gaulle and Adolf Hitler
   were all leading personalities in the Second World War.
   e. They are all New Testament apostles.
   f. They are all architectural terms used in describing a
   vault or dome.
   g. All three words are general terms used to describe a
   period of time.
   h. All three words begin with 'tri', which signifies three.
   i. All three words describe different parts of a tree.
   j. All three words describe different types of bridge.
   k. All three words are types of accent on French letters.
   l. They are all employees in a household.

REASONING

1. Complete the missing numbers:

   a. 6520 – 7522 – 8524 – ?
   b. 9528 – 978 – 4214 – 434 – 8632 – 892 – 4218 – ?
   – 5627 – ? – 3270 – ? – 2240 – ?

2. Complete the missing numbers:

   10 – 11 – 21 – 12 – 600 – 612 – 5 – ? – 7 – 2 – ?
   – 14 – 2 – ? – 600 – 520 – ? – 521 –
   540 – 540 – ? – 12 – 2 – ? – 6 – ? – 600

3. Following the series indicated, complete the missing
   numbers:

   46 – 604 – 406 – 12 – 201 – 102 – 27 – ? – 207 –
   11 – ? – ? – 98 – ? – ?

4. Complete the following series by writing in the missing letters:

J – J – A – S – O – N – ? – ? – ? – ? – ? – ?

5. Continue the series already started, as shown in the first two examples, by filling in the dominoes and marking the necessary number of points on the scoring board:

I	II	III
2	5	4
6	4	8
4 + 3	8 - 6	9 - 1

IV	V	VI
6	9	11
3	9	3
4 x 2	20 + 21	5 + 4

6. Replace the bold numbers with the appropriate letters:
   19 – T – U – D – **19** – D – E – F – **25** – S – T –
   O – **16** – A – B – **19** – C – **5** – **19** – **19** – S – T –
   A – **13** – **16**

7. Complete the missing numbers:
   99 – 198 – 296 – 393 – 489 – ? – ? – ? – ?

8. Complete the missing letters:
   M – N – L – O – K – P – J – Q – ? – ? – ? – ? –
   ? – ?

9. Complete the missing letters and numbers:
   M 13 – N 13 – K 11 – P 11 – I 9 – R 9 – G 7 – T 7 –
   ? – ? – ? – ? – ? – ?

10. Complete the series shown by filling in the missing letters:
    220 B – 420 D – 51 E – 630 F – 820 H – 910 I – 10 J
    – 30 ? – 1 ? – 70 ? – 11 ? – 12 ?

Answers

1a. You will notice that, for each of the three numbers of four digits, the second and third digits (5 and 2) remain unchanged. Only the first and last increase each time in a consistent way – by 1 and 2 respectively (i.e. by 1002). The missing number, therefore, is: 8524 + 1002 = **9526**.

1b. You can see the succession of numbers with four and then three digits in 'pairs'. For each pair, the first and last digit of each number remain the same. If you look at the second digit of the three-figure number, this corresponds to the sum of the second and third digit of the previous four-figure number. The missing numbers, therefore, are: **438 – 587 – 390 – 260**.

2. You will see that the series is composed of groups of three numbers, the third being the sum of the previous two. The missing numbers are either the first, second or third in their respective group, the final figure being the total of the other two. The full series – with the missing numbers in bold – is therefore: 10 – 11 – 21 – 12 – 600 – 612 – 5 – **2** – 7 – 2 – **12** – 14 – 2 – **598** – 600 – 520 – **1** – 521 – 540 – 540 – **1080** – 12 – 2 – **14** – 6 – **594** – 600.

3. Here again the numbers are grouped in threes and you will see that, with each group, the middle number starts with the last digit of the first number and ends with the first digit of the last – with a 0 in the middle. The full series – with the missing numbers in bold – is therefore: 46 – 604 – 406 – 12 – 201 – 102 – 27 – **702** – 207 – 11 – **101** – **101** – 98 – **809** – **908**.

4. Each letter in the series corresponds, in order, to the initial letter of each month of the year, starting with June. The missing letters are therefore:
    D – J – F – M – A – M.

5. Each figure presents five sets of numbers arranged vertically. The third is obtained through the simple operation of adding or subtracting as indicated. The last two sets of numbers – on the dominoes and the scoring board – are the ones to be found. You will see that if you multiply the first two numbers together and then subtract from this the third number, you will arrive at the fourth (on the domino). When this equals or is more than 12 (i.e. double-six on a domino), it is divided by two. The fifth number (on the scoring board) is obtained by subtracting the first number from the fourth. The missing numbers (on the dominoes and scoring boards respectively) are therefore: Fig III: **6 & 2** – Fig IV: **10 & 4** – Fig V: **10 & 1** – Fig VI: **6 & 5**.

6. Here the numbers in bold correspond, in numerical order, to the letters of the alphabet (i.e. **S** is the 19th letter in the alphabet). By replacing the numbers with their corresponding letters, you will make up five words as follows: STUDS – DEFY – STOP – ABSCESS – STAMP.

7. With this series of numbers you will see that the value of each increases progressively and constantly by the following amount: + 100, then -1; + 100, then – 2 etc. The missing numbers are therefore:
584 – 678 – 771 – 863.

8. You will notice that the letters M and N which begin the series are the two middle letters of the alphabet, the 13th and 14th respectively. The series continues in the same way, coupling the 12th and 15th letters, the 11th and 16th and so on. The missing letters are therefore:
I – R – H – S – G – T.

9. Note here that the same value number is attributed to each couple of letters, which are classed as in the previous question (i.e. MN, KP, IR etc). The series progresses in a decreasing order for the first letter of each pair and in an increasing order for the second, following the alphabetical order and jumping a letter each time. The common value attributed to each couple of letters is that affected by the first letter of each pair, following the order of the letters of the alphabet (a = 1, b = 2, c = 3 etc). The correct answers are therefore:
E 5 – V 5 – C 3 – X 3 – A 1 – Z 1.

10. Here you have a succession of numbers to which a letter is attributed each time. You will notice that the 2nd, 3rd, 4th, 5th, 6th and 7th numbers are given letters that go in alphabetical order. The first digit of each number increases in the same way and is equivalent to the numerical place of the accompanying letter in the alphabet – B = 2, D = 4, E = 5, F = 6 etc. The missing letters (in bold) are therefore:
30 C – 1 A – 70 G – 11 K – 12 L.

VERBAL COMPREHENSION

1. Choose the definition that you think best applies to the following words:

a. ATHEIST
Who does not believe in God.
Who has lost the faith.
Who does not practise any religion.

b. BIMONTHLY
Which takes place twice every quarter.
Which takes place every four months.
Which takes place every two months.

c. BALLOT
Action of counting the voting papers.
Vote cast by means of voting papers.
The results of a vote.

d. POSTPONE
To send later.
To put off till a later date.
To send back.

2. Indicate the verb of action that you think best describes each of the following propositions (only one verb for each):

   a. He entered the house like a cat in order to steal all he could find there.
   b. The army established itself on the outskirts of the town.
   c. We went to study the ground.

3. Indicate two verbs of action that you think are synonymous with each of the verbs used in the following propositions:

   a. He left all his competitors behind.
   b. He left the front door partly open.

4. Put the words that appear in the following columns in pairs, according to their sense or association:

Gramme	Weight	Awkward	Date
Bosnia	Number	John Major	Pence
Robot	Punishment	Walter Scott	Mischievous
Graham Greene	Automatic	Clumsy	Penalty
Edward Heath	Addition	Sarajevo	Lead
Nation	Charity	La	Collar

History	Ecu	Deputy	So
French	Senator	Donation	Russian
Novel	Troublesome	Toga	Tunic
Friend	Book	People	Brother

5. Couple up the words that appear in the following columns to create another word (with or without a hyphen) in common use:
   Example: Week and End = Weekend

Strap	Watch	Cross	After
Place	Cordon	Wishing	Half
Bleu	Lamp	See	States
Saw	Thought	Shade	Anti
Market	Body	Red	Well
Seam	Bread	Tease	Long
Awake	Man	Winner	Four
Word	Stress	Guard	Fire
Iron	Wrought	Fur	Breast
Step	Twenty	Strip	Door

Answers

1a. ATHEIST – **Who does not believe in God.**
1b. BIMONTHLY – **Which takes place every two months.**
1c. BALLOT – **Vote cast by means of voting papers.**
1d. POSTPONE – **To put off till a later date.**

2. The verbs of action are (in order): **burgle – encamp – prospect.**

3. The two verbs of action synonymous with the two propositions are:

   a. outpace & outstrip.
   b. half-open & leave ajar.

4. The list of words pair up as follows:

Gramme – Weight	Awkward – Clumsy
Date – History	Bosnia – Sarajevo
Number – Addition	John Major – Edward Heath
Coin – Ecu	Robot – Automatic

Punishment – Penalty Walter Scott – Graham Greene
Mischievous – Troublesome Lead – Collar
Nation – People Charity – Donation
La – So Deputy – Senator
French – Russian Novel – Book
Toga – Tunic Friend – Brother

5. The list of words couple up as follows:

Watch-strap Crossword
After-thought Marketplace
Cordon-bleu Wishing-well
Half-awake Lampshade
Seesaw Statesman
Antibody Redbreast
Seamstress Bread-winner
Striptease Furlong
Twenty-four Fireguard
Wrought-iron Doorstep

WRITTEN AND ORAL EXPRESSIONS

1a. Underline in the following series the words where the **a** is pronounced as in **hate, relate,** etc.

mare – maze – tall – tale – page – raw – rare – gate – pane – far – blame – saw – sag – sage – pageant – favourite – harm – phrase – ancient – arm – tame – trap – later – latter

1b. Underline in the following series the words where the **ig** is pronounced as in **right, benign,** etc.

height – weight – sight – weigh – high – eight – feign – flight – sigh – prig – light – reign – slight – sign – signet – align – assign – fig – fight – plight – malign – malignant

2a. Underline in the following series those words having a common root of **no/non** as a negative.

none – nominate – nobody – now – innocent – nonentity – nought – innocuous – nonsense – nondescript – know – novel – nowhere – notorious – nonconformist – notable – annotate – nothing – agnostic – nonetheless.

2b. Underline in the following series those words having the common root of **leg** with a legal connotation.

elegant – illegal – legislate – illegible – legion – illegitimate – allegory – legalist – delegate – legality – legitimacy – allegro – legend – legislation – college – legislature – legalise – telegram – elegy – legalism.

3. Find the word of two (or three) syllables corresponding to each of the following sentences from the syllables in the two columns on the right.

a. He can crunch with his teeth	BI	SI
b. Those stacks of newspaper were put there	STA	RA
c. You are going to dirty your suit	ME	TA
d. This problem can be solved without difficulty	LY	DE
(3 syllables)	TE	PID
e. This exercise is done in just five minutes	IN	PI
(3 syllables)	EA	LE

4. In the following sentences, select the missing word(s) from the three given that seems to you to be correct.

a. I gave them .... books back. (there/their/theirs)

b. I'd like .... information you've got about holidays in Greece. (an/some/any)

c. I lived there .... three years. (for/since/during)

d. He must .... by now. (be arrived/arrive/have arrived)

e. Has she phoned ....? (soon/already/now)

f. She .... her jewellery for £15,000. (assured/ensured/insured)

g. Their house was built .... the hill. (on top of/above/over)

Answers

1a. maze – tale – page – gate – pane – blame – sage – favourite – phase – ancient – tame – later.

1b. height – sight – high – flight – sigh – light – slight – sign – align – assign – fight – plight – malign.

2a. none – nobody – nonentity – nought – nonsense – nondescript – nowhere – nonconformist – nothing – nonetheless.

2b. illegal – legislate – illegitimate – legalist – legality – legitimacy – legislation – legislature – legalise – legalism.

3. The words from the syllables listed are:

    a. BI – TE
    b. PI – LE
    c. STA – IN
    d. EA – SI – LY
    e. RA – PID – LY

4.   **a.** their
    b. any
    c. for
    d. have arrived
    e. already
    f. insured
    g. on top of

2.   Personality tests

THE EGO TEST

Choose from the following sentences, in groups of five or six, those that seem to you to correspond best with your personality, marking with a cross just one in each group:

1. I cannot be happy when so many people are suffering.
    I want to be happy.
    I do not feel guilty being happy.
    I feel I have the right to be happy.
    I would like all the world to be happy.
    It is impossible to be happy on this earth.

2. I have never had what I wanted.
    I can have what I want.
    I want what I do not have.
    I cannot have what I want.
    I want what I cannot have.
    I do not want what I cannot have.

3. I have what I deserve.
    I do not deserve what I have.
    I have not had what I deserved.
    One always deserves more than one has.
    I have had what I deserved.
    One only has what one deserves.

4. One can cheat and not be found out.
    There are rules one must respect.
    One must do one's duty.
    Rules must be the same for all.
    One should know what one wants.

5. I look particularly like my mother.
    I look particularly like my father.
    I do not look like anyone.
    I do not look like either.
    I look like both.

6. One must be respectful.

I am not respected.
I know how to be respectful.
Those who do not respect you should be punished.
Each has the right to due respect.

7. I always accept my responsibilities.
   I am particularly generous.
   I can be considered mean.
   I ask for a lot.
   I know my limits.

8. I can pretend.
   I do not know how to pretend.
   I do not like pretending.
   Sometimes I pretend.
   I pretend when I have to.
   I do not like people who pretend.

9. I know I am considered knowledgeable.
   Knowledge is not enough.
   I am not sure about my knowledge.
   Sometimes I lack ability.
   One cannot know everything.
   I know more than I have to.

10. I often feel uneasy.
    I feel particularly at ease.
    I can easily put myself at ease.
    I do not like people who take it easy.
    One cannot always be at ease.

11. I know how to frighten if I have to.
    It is dangerous to be afraid.
    I can appear not to be afraid.
    I am not a timid person.
    Sometimes I can be afraid.
    I do not frighten anyone.

Interpretation

This test sets out to examine different pathological tendencies in one's personality, the repercussions of which

on one's professional activities and social relationships could prove problematic.

This test is measured on the basis of four main tendencies, which include a scale on deceit or delusion, as well as a small group of items considered 'neutral' which are also taken into account in the final analysis.

Each 'tendency' is defined by a certain number of items considered to represent it.

The N Tendency
I feel I have the right to be happy.
I can have what I want.
I have what I deserve (N+).
or
I have had what I deserved (N-).
There are rules one must respect (N-).
or
One should know what one wants (N+).
I look like both.
I know how to be respectful (N+).
or
Each has the right to due respect (N-).
I know my limits.
Sometimes I pretend.
I know I am considered knowledgeable (N+).
or
One cannot know everything (N-).
I feel particularly at ease (N+).
or
One cannot always be at ease (N-).
Sometimes I can be afraid.

The PP Tendency
It is impossible to be happy on this earth.
I want what I do not have (PP+).
or
I want what I cannot have (PP-).
I do not deserve what I have.
One can cheat and not be found out.
I look particularly like my mother (*if the candidate is male*).
I look particularly like my father (*if the candidate is female*).

I pretend when I have to.
One must be respectful.
I can be considered mean (PP+).
or
I ask for a lot (PP-).
Knowledge is not enough.
I can easily put myself at ease.
It is dangerous to be afraid (PP-).
or
I can appear not to be afraid (PP+).

The D Tendency
I cannot be happy when so many people are suffering (D+).
or
I would like all the world to be happy (D-).
I cannot have what I want (D+).
or
I have never had what I wanted (D-).
One always deserves more than one has (D-).
or
I have not had what I deserved (D+).
Rules must be the same for all.
I do not look like either.
I am not respected.
I am particularly generous.
I do not know how to pretend (D+).
I do not like pretending (D-).
or
I am not sure about my knowledge (D+).
I often feel uneasy.
I do not frighten anyone.

The P Tendency
I do not feel guilty being happy.
I do not want what I cannot have.
One only has what one deserves.
One must do one's duty.
I do not look like anyone.
Those who do not respect you should be punished.
I always accept my responsibilities (*see **HM Scale**).
I do not like people who pretend.

I know more than I have to.
I do not like people who take it easy.
I know how to frighten if I have to.

HM Scale (deceit scale)
I know my limits.
Sometimes I pretend.
(The presence of these two items can be considered as a favourable indication of the sincerity of the candidate.)
I always accept my responsibilities.
(When this item appears among those considered by the candidate, one can take this as a desire to be seen in the best possible light or infer from it the P Tendency, if the choice of other items matches this hypothesis.)

Neutral items
I want to be happy.
I look like my mother *(if the candidate is female).*
I look like my father *(if the candidate is male).*
I can pretend.
I am not a timid person.

No particular value is attached to these five items which, if it proves necessary for the final interpretation, can be counted as items under the N Tendency. To be correctly assessed, the answer paper must contain eleven items chosen by the candidate (one item per group as requested).

The interpretation consists of putting each item chosen by the candidate with the tendency to which it matches. When more than seven of the possible eleven items appear under the same tendency (N, P, PP or D), that tendency is then considered valid.

If the spread of replies is too diverse (less than six or seven items under the same tendency), then a valid interpretation is impossible.

The consistency of the replies or, conversely, the incoherence or contradiction that appears in the choice of items is equally considered as significant.

The N Tendency (norm)
This tendency does not need much in the way of comment. The subject seems happy to be in the world, balanced in her

professional activities and in her social relationships.
* N+ indicates a strong and narcissistic ego.
* N- suggests a more flexible and moderate subject, more 'socialised' in her attitudes.

The deceit scale (HM) and the neutral items enable the examiner to adjust his interpretation depending on the general appreciation of the candidate during the test and in relation to the other items given as answers.

The D Tendency (depressive state)

The D Tendency shows up as a sadness that can go as far as depression or significant moral anguish. Such suffering is born by the candidate as a failure or doubt concerning one's own value. Communication is established, but on a negative plane. There can be an agreeable and disagreeable side to a persons emotional and social state, without ever reaching an equilibrium.

Such disguised states of depression, which are often hard to detect, can affect one's professional activities. The repercussions on the interest the subject can find in the outside world are considerable, depending on the seriousness of the inhibition. This tendency corresponds to the ideas of social injustice, even to the loss of a taste for living.

All this adds up to a feeling of failure which is difficult to detect from the outside but enough to upset the relative equilibrium of the subject. The D+ Tendency indicates a fragile ego, which results in a certain difficulty in finding satisfaction in the real world.

The P Tendency (paranoiac ego)

The P Tendency marks egocentricity and exaggerated self-esteem, intolerance and the contempt of others, with conceit capable of going as far as megalomania, and a relative intolerance to frustration.

Inflexibility, mistrust and an exaggerated sensitivity to criticism derive from a self-confidence sufficiently fragile as to need reassurance and underline the jealous temperament of the subject.

The PP Tendency

The PP Tendency is determined by the convergence of several elements: open or disguised aggression, the imbalance and immaturity of the psychopath or pervert, which expresses itself in sadomasochistic tendencies, the need to make others (or oneself) suffer, delusion and impulsiveness. Inadaptibility is combined with a sense of despair or a conception of a particularly dark world.

The desire for and the anguish from destruction, the lack of moral sense and the instability can all lead the subject to verbal abuse or criminal activity and a progressive desocialisation.

Practical advice

It is clear that the results obtained from this test should be interpreted with the greatest possible reserve. And this goes for all the tests or questionnaires concerning 'personality' presented in this book, which only offers a summary or résumé of a proper test under real examination conditions.

Moreover, it is important to underline the fact that, if one wants to obtain conclusive results, this type of exercise must be controlled by specialists.

THE QUOTATION TEST

With each of the following propositions, indicate with a tick in the relevant box whether you feel it is **true**, **false** or **uncertain**:

	True	False	Uncertain
1. A tree is born to break and not to bend.	☐	☐	☐
2. Practice is the only theory that profits.	☐	☐	☐
3. Obedience and use of reason are what make up true Christianity.	☐	☐	☐
4. We always end up despising those who agree with us too easily.	☐	☐	☐
5. All success hides surrender.	☐	☐	☐
6. Trust of the young elevates the man of character.	☐	☐	☐
7. The greatest devotion should not			

	True	False	Uncertain
get in the way of business.	☐	☐	☐
8. Man is not made to be guilty.	☐	☐	☐
9. Man does not live by bread alone.	☐	☐	☐
10. I do not like work, no-one does; but I like what is involved in work, the chance to discover oneself.	☐	☐	☐
11. All means are good if they are effective.	☐	☐	☐
12. I consider myself responsible; others, never.	☐	☐	☐
13. Everyone is responsible for everything.	☐	☐	☐
14. It is always easy to obey if one dreams of commanding.	☐	☐	☐
15. All reasoning amounts to giving in to sentiment.	☐	☐	☐
16. We always need to make someone responsible for our troubles and misfortunes.	☐	☐	☐
17. For me happiness is not so much doing what I want but not doing what I don't want.	☐	☐	☐
18. Pleasure can only be appreciated among those who share the benefit.	☐	☐	☐
19. One doesn't do what one wants, yet one is responsible for what one is.	☐	☐	☐
20. He who obeys is almost always better than he who commands.	☐	☐	☐
21. Real men of progress are those who have from the start a deep respect for the past.	☐	☐	☐
22. No man has a natural right to rule over others.	☐	☐	☐
23. Generous people make bad businessmen.	☐	☐	☐
24. For me, real courage is caution.	☐	☐	☐
25. The wise man's way is without fighting.	☐	☐	☐
26. Missed vocations affect one's whole life.	☐	☐	☐

	True	False	Uncertain

27. Obedience is the most perfect science. ☐ ☐ ☐

28. The characteristic of orthodoxy is not to be affected by those who dominate. ☐ ☐ ☐

29. People who want something badly enough are nearly always best served by chance. ☐ ☐ ☐

30. Authority is not so much the quality of a man as a relationship between two human beings. ☐ ☐ ☐

31. To search is not one thing and to find another, but the reward from the search is the search itself. ☐ ☐ ☐

32. The proof of the pudding is in the eating. ☐ ☐ ☐

33. There isn't a society. A society in itself is neither virtuous nor bad, wise nor foolish; it exists. ☐ ☐ ☐

34. The woman who does a man's work belongs to a third sex. ☐ ☐ ☐

35. The court is a sacred place where everyone must keep under control the two betrayers they cannot overcome: speech and expression. ☐ ☐ ☐

36. A nation needs someone who understands its desire, epitomises it and takes it where it must go. ☐ ☐ ☐

37. Coolness is the greatest quality of a man destined to lead. ☐ ☐ ☐

38. Success is the only justification for rebellion. ☐ ☐ ☐

39. Society exists for the benefit of man and not man for the benefit of society. ☐ ☐ ☐

40. Where you have been servant, do not be master. ☐ ☐ ☐

41. When you want to manage people, you shouldn't lead from the front but follow from behind. ☐ ☐ ☐

True False Uncertain

42. Don't consider anything as favourable that can cost you your self-respect.

43. Nature has made man happy and good, but society corrupts and makes him miserable.

44. A great person does well enough for us when he doesn't do us any harm.

45. It is better to win by chance than with one's sword or beauty.

46. To react with strength one needs a touch of humility.

47. It is events which direct men and not men who direct events.

48. One must bend in order to pick up.

49. One goes at a steadier pace by following than by leading.

50. If you can't push, then pull; if you can't pull, then get out.

Interpretation

This test, which could be put in the category of those concerning temperament, attempts to expose two tendencies: the ability to take command and the direction and ability in both execution and obedience.

Two sub-scales, as well as the groups of items (i.e. the propositions and sentences), which are classed as CI, SI and AI, are used to refine this perception through the particular nuances they carry.

The A and B groups each epitomise two different types of temperament.

Group A defines the robust and hard individuals, with an authoritative temperament, realistic and independent, relying on thought and judgement, especially designated for management, the organisation of work and the taking of responsibility.

Group B involves more flexible individuals, malleable,

sensitive or modest, dependant and particularly given to the task of execution.

Association with Group A or B is made if the candidate has replied favourably to at least fifteen of the items representing that tendency.

The A Tendency: Items 1 – 4 – 6 – 7 – 8 – 10 – 11 – 14 – 17 – 19 – 23 – 26 – 28 – 29 – 30 – 32 – 36 – 37 – 39 – 40 – 41 – 45 – 47 – 50.
The B Tendency: Items 3 – 5 – 12 – 13 – 15 – 16 – 18 – 20 – 21 – 24 – 25 – 27 – 30 – 31 – 32 – 34 – 36 – 37 – 38 – 43 – 44 – 46 – 48 – 49.

Formal items
Each of the items listed below help to confirm either the A or B Tendency. For either tendency to be endorsed, the candidate must have replied favourably to at least ten of these items.

The A Tendency: Items 1 – 4 – 6 – 7 – 8 – 11 – 17 – 19 – 26 – 28 – 29 – 30 – 32 – 36 – 37 – 41 – 45 – 47 – 50.
The B Tendency: Items 3 – 5 – 12 – 13 – 15 – 18 – 20 – 21 – 24 – 25 – 27 – 32 – 34 – 36 – 37 – 38 – 44 – 46 – 48 – 49.

Sub-scales: AA & BB
If the candidates of Group A replied 'yes' to Items 22 and 30, as well as Items 42 and 47, then they can be considered as negotiators and persuaders.

If the candidates of Group B replied 'yes' to Items 13 and 15, as well as Items 18, 20, 42 and 43, then they are sensitive, of sociable spirit, flexible yet firm on certain principles. If they replied 'yes' to Item 46 and 'no' to Items 38 and 11, their tendency can be that of a social worker or can equally well represent a union delegate or orthodox militant.

Sensitive items
If the candidates belonging to Group A replied 'yes' to Items 11, 1 and 8, the tendency to dominate is very marked. It can add up to an unstable individual, a 'dare-devil', little given to scruples and with difficulty in socialising – the Aa Tendency.

If the candidates belonging to Group B replied 'no' or

'uncertain' to Items 22, 47 and 41, this is known as the Bb Tendency. This sub-group includes people for whom trust in and respect for authority can lead to fanaticism and blind obedience. Work fulfilment and social relations in general are seen as a mythical scale through which authority is given an almost divine status. This tendency is largely confirmed if the B candidates reply 'yes' to Items 44, 4 and 39. Trust and self-sacrifice can thus commit them to the role of sucker or consenting slave.

Common items
The CI scale groups six items regarded as 'sensitive' – namely 6, 32, 37, 30, 36 and 50 – and refers equally as well to Group A as to Group B. The replies given to each of these six items enable the examiner to judge the candidate's attitude towards hierarchy and respect for authority, whatever the retained dominant tendency (A or B) and the sense of adhesion and team spirit of the candidate.

The tendency is valid if the candidate has replied 'yes' to four of the six items.

Super-ego items
This scale (SI), like the previous one independent of the A or B Tendency, groups five items (8, 11, 33, 35 and 42) which highlight a particular aspect of what one could call moral or ethical sense, judgement and respect for the law or social rules which derive from it.

For this tendency to be valid, one needs to have replied 'yes' to Item 42 and 'no' or 'uncertain' to the others.

The All Tendency
This tendency involves the most independent individuals, unclassifiable or declassified, anarchists or fiercely individualistic. It can also signal on the part of the candidates a total rejection of the conditions of the test – or simply their exception to it, if the moral sense is maintained. (In this case, see **Super-ego items**.)

For this tendency to be valid, candidates must have replied 'yes' to between nine and eleven items classed under Group A or B and not have included more than five 'sensitive' items in the series (see **Sensitive items Aa & Bb**).

Practical advice

Note on a piece of paper all the items to which you have replied 'yes' and all those to which you have replied 'no'. Repeat the exercise for the sub-scales AA and BB, the sensitive items, the common items and the super-ego items. Reading through all these items in turn can prove instructive if you succeed in distinguishing some of the sensitive points or those that strike you as interesting to highlight.

THE SOCIAL EXPRESSION TEST

Reply as quickly as possible, in no more than three lines each time, putting yourself in the situations described here and as if you had the person speaking in front of you. Each reply must be a direct one.

1. You are on the point of leaving on holiday. Your boss tells you that some urgent work must be finished in the next few days. Your departure is threatened. *You reply:* "...

2. You are called in to see your boss. He proposes moving you to a job previously held by one of your friends, who was fired the day before. *You reply:* "...

3. A jealous colleague comes to congratulate you on the promotion you have just earned. *You reply:* "...

4. You are involved in a meeting with all the company's managers. One of your colleagues stands up and says that your presence of mind has happily got the group out of a difficult situation. *You reply:* "...

5. A job that has to be finished keeps you at the office after six o'clock with other colleagues. One of them remarks that your negligence is to blame for the delay. *You reply:* "...

6. You happen to pass with flying colours an exam for which you have worked very hard. You are entitled to the congratulations of the examiners. *You reply:* "...

7. You happen to end up in a job where the employees

who arrive late pass in the lift those who are leaving early. The boss asks you how you are getting on in your new work. *You reply: "...*

8. One of your colleagues at work does not stop making mistakes. You are reprimanded for the subsequent poor results. *You reply: "...*

9. A colleague for whom you have already left several messages has not called you back. You must contact him since the matter is urgent. He apologises for not having got back to you earlier. *You reply: "...*

10. You are on the way to achieving an enviable position at work. Some colleagues criticise you for your ambition. *You reply: "...*

11. Your boss arrives late for a meeting and asks you to give him your seat. *You reply: "...*

12. You have promised your support for a colleague in a delicate situation. Then you happen to learn of another solution preferred by the management which puts pressure on you. The colleague asks you to make your position clear. *You reply: "...*

13. You happen to end up in a difficult company for whom you have not always performed to the best of your ability. You are asked to go back over all your work. *You reply: "...*

14. You are in charge of a complicated dossier. You discuss your point of view with your boss who recommends another course of action. *You reply: "...*

15. You happen to rise to a position of responsibility for which you have worked hard. Your best friend calls to find out the news. *You reply: "...*

16. One of your colleagues, who is less competent than yourself, gets promoted. He arrives to tell you about it. *You reply: "...*

17. You are in the process of finishing some urgent work. A client, who has not made an appointment, asks to see you. *You reply: "...*

18. You are told that you have been given a difficult job to do which will inconvenience your family but for which you will be well-paid. *You reply:* "...

19. A business associate apologises on your behalf for missing a meeting. *You reply:* "...

20. You happen to learn about the mediocre results achieved by a colleague on a certain job. You have to give your opinion in front of her. *You reply:* "...

21. One of your colleagues deliberately manages to block your moves to obtain some professional advantages. By chance you meet up and she asks you if you have any news. *You reply:* "...

22. You happen to be given a management post with a team who miss your predecessor. On several occasions you have overheard her praises being sung. *You reply:* "...

23. A business associate whom you have excellent reason to dislike runs into some serious professional problems. She asks you to help her out. *You reply:* "...

Interpretation

The social expression test enables the examiner to study the behaviour and reactions of candidates faced with both failure and success. It also serves to highlight qualities of sociability in professional relations.

Five tendencies are involved in the types of response generally given to the situations presented above. Through these it will be possible to discern both overriding and underlying characteristics, which will be classified as A, SP, NA, SS and N. Example: an A/SP tendency means A is overriding and SP is underlying.

The R or RR scale, which is in addition to the five main tendencies described below, defines a favourable type of response – be it on reality and perception (R) or relational and emotional aspects (RR) – to each of the given situations.

The five tendencies

Reply A: AGGRESSION
The situation provokes the subject into an aggressive reaction, which exerts itself against another person, act or object.

Reply SP: SELF-PUNISHMENT
The subject's aggression is internally directed, so causing or inducing a feeling of responsibility for the situation.

Reply NA: NON-AGGRESSION
Aggressiveness is avoided or diverted and a kind of equilibrium is reached, depending on the situation described.

Reply SS: SELF-SATISFACTION
The subject's ego regards itself as sufficiently strong to be positive about the situation and to be in command of the different types of social happenings that arise. This attitude can also be qualified as voluntarist if it proves to be overriding in the results of the test.

Reply N: NEUTRAL TENDENCY
The subject does not get involved in conflict – or at least does not appear to – and overcomes difficulties through restraint or tactical manoeuvring.

Examples

Here are a few examples which will illustrate the type of replies possible (A, SP, NA, SS or N), depending on the situation encountered, and the R or RR classification it carries.

Item 3: *A jealous colleague comes to congratulate you...*

Reply A: "Thank you for making the effort to appear sincere." (RR)

Reply SP: "I wasn't expecting such a promotion." (R)

Reply NA: "I will do my best to get on top of the job." (R)

Reply SS: "I am very pleased. I have been rewarded for my efforts." (R) **or**
"Thank you for the pleasure (or honour) you have given me." (RR)

Reply N: "Thank you." (R or RR)

Item 11: *Your boss arrives late for a meeting...*
Reply A: "Go and find your own!" (RR)
Reply SP: "Please forgive me..." (RR)
Reply NA: "I'll go and find another one." (R)
Reply SS: "It's an honour for me give up my seat to someone like you." (R) **or**
"Willingly. Do sit down." (RR)
Reply N: "Please do sit down." (RR)

Item 14: *You are in charge of a complicated dossier...*
Reply A: "You could have told me that before." (RR)
Reply SP: "I realise I did not choose the right method." (R)
Reply NA: "I hadn't thought of that." (R)
Reply SS: "I am very satisfied we have the situation well in hand." (RR)
Reply N: "I see what you mean." (RR)

Item 21: *You happen to learn of the mediocre results...*
Reply A: "As far as she is concerned, that doesn't surprise me." (RR)
Reply SP: "I'm not sure I could have done any better." (R)
Reply NA: "It's not an easy job." (R)
Reply SS: "It's now or never to succeed." (RR) **or**
"I am sure my colleague will put it right." (RR)
Reply N: "It must be done differently." (R)

Practical advice

Here the tendencies amount to five. By counting the number of A, SP, NA, SS and N replies, one can discover the overriding and underlying tendencies and the accompanying R or RR classification. The highest number of replies belonging to a single series determines the overriding tendency.

Uncertain replies (R or RR)

Count the number of R or RR replies, that is to say the number of uncertain responses which can belonging to either series. Divide this number by two and distribute one half in R and the other in RR.

Double replies

Here is an example. "It is not your fault, but you should have been more careful." or "It is not an easy job, but I am sure my colleague will put it right."

The first proposition ("It is not your fault...") should be marked as NA – RR*, with the second part ("...but you should have been more careful.") as A – RR*.

The second proposition ("It is not an easy job...") should be marked as NA – R*, with the second part (...but I am sure my colleague will put it right.") as SS – RR*.

The asterisk indicates that one has to deal with a double reply which is going to alter the results as a whole. A significant number of double replies signals a form of contradiction and a personality with a tendency to work on two levels or one which finds itself searching for an inner balance.

THE T9 MOTIVATION TEST

Mark with a tick four of the following activities, classing them in order of preference (i.e. 1, 2, 3 and 4):

I   You prefer:
   1. To work outdoors.
   2. To make things.
   3. To express or create.
   4. To make telephone calls or organise meetings.
   5. To write news stories or articles.
   6. To make scientific discoveries.
   7. To win over an audience.
   8. To arouse and captivate.
   9. To observe natural phenomena.
   10. To organise a fashion show.
   11. To work in a hospital or laboratory.
   12. To draw up a balance-sheet or manage a portfolio.
   13. To manipulate ideas or concepts.
   14. To draw up plans or diagrams.
   15. To sort out figures and analyse them.
   16. To handle and touch.

II A. You prefer to spend your free afternoons (*tick just one of the following*):

1. Doing jobs around the home.
2. Reading encyclopaedias.
3. Going on outings.
4. Visiting the cinema or museums.

B. You would like to learn more about *(tick just one of the following)*:
1. The human body, the universe, matter.
2. Foreign languages, geography.
3. Law, psychology, societies.
4. Computers, mechanics, optics.

C. Some friends move to a house in the country and ask you to give them a hand. You prefer *(tick just one of the following)*:
1. To check the electrical wiring.
2. To organise the furnishings in the sitting-room.
3. Unpack the boxes.
4. Prepare a good meal.

D. You would prefer to learn by heart *(tick just one of the following)*:
1. An extract from a piece of literature.
2. A sales contract.
3. The list of British counties or the Highway Code.
4. A piece of music.

III From the contrasting characteristics listed below, underline the five words that seem to you to correspond best with your personality:
   1. Imaginative or planning.
   2. Emotional or cold.
   3. Sprinter or stayer.
   4. Trusting or mistrusting.
   5. Resolute or anxious.
   6. Sociable or discreet.
   7. Critical or satisfied.
   8. Authoritarian or flexible.
   9. Rushed or patient.
   10. Logical or sensitive.
   11. Innovative or cautious.
   12. Direct or evasive.

13. Slow or quick.
14. Dependant or independent.
15. Open or reserved.
16. Persuasive or quiet.
17. Organised or muddle-headed.
18. Observant or inattentive.
19. Concrete or abstract.
20. Intuitive or methodical.

IV. From the items listed below, underline five pairs of words that you feel correspond best with your personality:
 1. Sensual and intuitive.
 2. Calculating and methodical.
 3. Direct and spontaneous.
 4. Fantasizing and original.
 5. Conformist and reasonable.
 6. Cold and detached.
 7. Practical and concrete.
 8. Curious and imaginative.
 9. Well-ordered and fastidious.
10. Patient and quiet.
11. Reformist and organising.
12. Enterprising and realistic.
13. Direct and outspoken.
14. Trusting and relaxed.
15. Discreet and efficient.
16. Modest and conscientious.
17. Bold and resourceful.
18. Opportunist and cunning.
19. Perfectionist and accurate.
20. Manual and physical.

V Tick just four of the following activities, classifying them in order of preference (i.e. 1, 2, 3 and 4):
 1. To observe and analyse.
 2. To conceive and realise.
 3. To test and feel.
 4. To make and construct.
 5. To speak and explain.
 6. To express and create.
 7. To repair and adapt.
 8. To reason and count.

9. To exercise and take a break.
10. To understand and help.
11. To arrange and classify.
12. To convince and argue.
13. To do and act.
14. To calculate and work out.
15. To listen and guide.
16. To summarise and pass on.
17. To plan and organise.
18. To deduce and apply.

Interpretation

This test aims at examining certain personality tendencies through different aspects of choice and privileged social interest. There are four tendencies involved here: introversion, extroversion, analysis and intuition.

The social choices indicate ability or interest over a wide field – artistic, scientific, manual, physical, numerical and verbal. This test can therefore be used to determine a career or professional orientation, depending on individual preferences and abilities.

I.   The candidate should have indicated here four choices of proposition in order of preference – 1, 2, 3 and 4. Each of the twenty items corresponds to an orientation or interest, be it artistic, physical, verbal or numerical. Here, as per the order given above, is the corresponding professional choice for each proposition:

1. Physical	2. Physical (mechanical)
3. Artistic	4. Verbal (persuasive)
5. Verbal	6. Numerical (scientific)
7. Verbal (persuasive)	8. Artistic
9. Physical (scientific)	10. Artistic (aesthetic)
11. Numerical (scientific)	12. Numerical
13. Verbal	14. Numerical (aesthetic)
15. Numerical	16. Physical

II   The second part of the test involves the same elements as the previous one under a different form.

A 1. Physical   **2.** Numerical (scientific)
  3. Physical   **4.** Artistic

B 1. Numerical (scientific)   **2.** Verbal
  3. Verbal (persuasive)   **4.** Numerical (mechanical)

C 1. Physical (mechanical)   **2.** Artistic (aesthetic)
  3. Physical   **4.** Physical

D 1. Verbal   **2.** Verbal (persuasive)
  3. Numerical   **4.** Artistic

III This part of the test proposes an examination of different personality tendencies: introversion, extroversion, analysis (reasoning, judgement, abstracts) or intuition (feelings, sensations, actuality). Here are the assessments for each pair of words in the order in which they appeared above:

1. Intuitive or analytic
2. Extrovert or introvert
3. Extrovert or introvert
4. Extrovert or introvert
5. Extrovert or introvert
6. Extrovert or introvert
7. Analytic or intuitive
8. Extrovert or introvert
9. Analytic or introvert
10. Analytic or introvert
11. Intuitive or analytic
12. Extrovert or introvert
13. Introvert or extrovert
14. Intuitive or analytic
15. Extrovert or introvert
16. Extrovert or introvert
17. Analytic or intuitive
18. Analytic or intuitive
19. Intuitive or analytic
20. Intuitive or analytic

IV This part of the test involves the same elements as the previous one, but under a different form. Here is the assessment attributed to each pair of words in the order in which they appeared above.

1. Intuitive	2. Analytic	3. Extrovert
4. Intuitive	5. Analytic	6. Introvert
7. Intuitive	8. Intuitive	9. Analytic
10. Introvert	11. Analytic	12. Analytic
13. Extrovert	14. Introvert	15. Introvert
16. Introvert	17. Extrovert	18. Intuitive
19. Analytic	20. Intuitive	

V   For this last set of questions, the candidate should have marked, in order of preference (1, 2, 3 and 4), four choices of activities. Each of the eighteen items corresponds to a particular orientation or professional interest: scientific, verbal, technical, numerical, physical, artistic, literary, social or the equivalent of office work. Here, in the order they appeared above, are the assessments corresponding to each proposition.

1. Scientific	2. Verbal (persuasive)	3. Artistic
4. Mechanical	5. Verbal (persuasive)	6. Artistic
7. Technical	8. Numerical	9. Physical
10. Social	11. Office work	12. Literary
13. Physical	14. Numerical	15. Social
16. Literary	17. Office work	18. Scientific

Each part of the test therefore comprises four or five items (or activities) that the candidate must have chosen as replies and, in certain cases, classed in order of preference.

It is then a question of regrouping these replies and defining, according to their number, an overriding or underlying tendency (extrovert, introvert, intuitive or analytic), continuing in the same way with the professional orientations indicated (scientific, literary, artistic, technical, etc). Each of the nine orientations mentioned here corresponds to a type of profession.

1. **Technical orientation:** manufacturer, fitter, electrician, mechanic, engineer, etc.
2. **Literary orientation:** school-teacher, translator, librarian, writer, proof-reader, journalist, editor, etc.
3. **Scientific orientation:** doctor, laboratory technician, biologist, pharmacist, chemist, engineer, etc.
4. **Verbal (persuasive) orientation:** public relations consultant, commercial director, insurer, company administra-

tor, trade unionist, personnel manager, publicity agent, etc.

5. **Artistic orientation:** all the arts, but also industrial painter, decorator, specialised animator, commercial designer, craftsman, etc.
6. **Physical orientation:** engineer or surveyor, forester, grower, mountain guide, gardener, physical education instructor, porter, shepherd, lorry driver, etc.
7. **Social service orientation:** psychologist, ergonomist, educational or professional counsellor, specialised nurse, social worker, educationalist, animator, school head, etc.
8. **Office work orientation:** typist, secretary, clerk, cashier, copyist, salesman, registrar, general office worker, etc.
9. **Numerical orientation:** accountant, statistician, bank employee, teacher, auditor, industrial engineer, sales manager, mathematician, economist, broker, etc.

The interpretation of the results of this test is going to enable the examiner to combine different types of profile, depending on the overriding and underlying tendencies exposed.

For example, scientific/physical orientation: forestry or water company engineer, meteorologist, site foreman, land surveyor, archaeologist or similar qualified profession. The choice will take into account the overriding and underlying tendencies (intuitive, analytic, introvert, extrovert) and should enable the examiner to make an accurate adjustment to the final interpretation, taking into account all the possible variants.

THE FIVE ELEMENTS TEST

With the help of these five elements, create three separate drawings, expressing yourself in the best way you can.

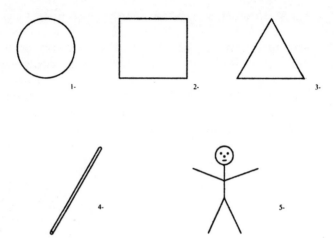

Interpretation

The test with the five elements is a project one, presenting candidates with a blank piece of paper on which they must draw their own images.

Naturally, on an empty sheet there will be a whole number of different possible concepts which will enable the examiner to study the objectified fantasies and a kind of topological representation of each candidate.

The initial hypothesis is as follows: there will be an organisation of the thought processes which will express themselves in some coherent form. The work of the psychologist is to recognise how each person's intelligence uses the invariants (circle, square, triangle, etc) to create individual themes or images.

A whole range of geometric combinations is possible. With these basic elements, candidates will use the space available subjectively to build up images, involving a thought process both structured and structuring, to which different meanings are going to be applied.

The picture idea (the mental image) that results from each drawing will enable the examiner to make an interpretation, from a whole series of themes which will be assimilated in the different images created.

The interpretation of each drawing will, of course, vary according to how the different images are assembled – for example, if two triangles are joined at their base or folded; if the square is used to create a series of right-angles; if a diamond is represented topped with a circle and so on.

The elements

1. THE CIRCLE
This is a complete, enclosed shape through which all traits pass without interruption. It expresses the idea of following some gesture and thought, of surrounding, bringing together, harmonising, synthetising. The circle represents the synthetic activity of intelligence, starting with and returning to sensitive intuition.

Geometric shapes, whether they are curved or straight lines, correspond by hypothesis to actions both real and virtual. Continuous and uninterrupted rhythms, the straight-line shapes are differentiated from curved-line ones because the subject attributes to them the existence of angles. These build up among others through perseverance, that is to say on several occasions.

2. THE RECTANGLE
This – or equally the square – is presented as a closed, elliptical shape and reveals active confrontation with the reality, vitality and pragmatism of the subject.

3. THE TRIANGLE
This is conceived as a property drawn directly on the object through a reconstruction, an appropriation. By interrupting from time to time thought and gesture – or even changing the direction in which he is drawing to master it – the subject's movement particularly characterizes the same process of assimilation (by the square circle) to know the mind. The curves and straight lines are supposed to represent symbolic forms.

4. THE STICK
This will be considered as an instrument of power or completeness and the image will be analysed on the basis of the

presence or absence of this one object, that is to say power or weakness symbolised by its inclusion or exclusion.

Aggression linked with pleasure against an object (represented in the drawing by a circle, square, etc) or the idea of private property or, on the contrary, the passive goal of yielding to pleasure through painful experiences are all different examples of how the elements are assessed, depending on how the subject uses the stick in his drawing.

Moreover it expresses, in the way the subject uses it, the need (and the means) to appear as an autonomous body, as much through obvious inhibition (for example, if the stick is lost or destroyed or missing) as in aggressive ambition. The object (the square, the circle, the triangle or even the little man) can be attacked or destroyed and return in the next drawing.

A person represented holding the stick in his hand indicates the predominance of the instinctive element, tension and vitality, constructive skills, discipline and educability.

5. THE LITTLE MAN
The opposition between active and passive is what will enable the analysis of the 'little man'. The dual active-passive sketches – to conquer or be conquered, to dominate or be dominated – correspond to a series of very specific pairs: kind/nasty, strong/weak, large/small...

Within the framework of this projective possibility (that is to say, through the drawing), the subject will express his feelings – whether it be the smallest, the largest, the strongest – depending on how he imagines himself. The dual, binary aspect is therefore the dimension that has been retained here, depending on the size of the figure in the drawing.

Depending on where the figure appears in the drawing (in the middle or to the left or right), the centripetal or centrifugal aspect is equally an essential co-ordinate in the interpretation, which will determine what element of narcissism there exists in the subject. The meanings attributed to the different positions will appear later, along with a few illustrations.

White space

The parts of the page remaining blank – or even the deliberate use of white space in the drawing – provide an additional dimension which will be included in the overall interpretation.

The area left without any drawings is significant according to whether it expresses a fundamental synthetic incapacity or is what remains of a crowded composition. It could be there are lines going out from a circle to create other figures, uniform squares and rectangles or, on the other hand, to relate with some other curved shapes, patches of space without anything, no person in the design... All these elements, strange or otherwise, will be taken into account in the final interpretation.

Therefore it is a question of analysing the exact use of the space, whether the overall image is scattered and unconnected or unified and elaborate.

The prevalence of converse images

These substitutive objects – the square, the triangle and the circle – will enable the examiner to build up the stages of a progression going from the merging relation to the image's conquest of its autonomous self.

This analysis is linked with the drawing of the little man in the space available and the use that is made of the stick. By observing the converse images – for example, a circle inside a square, the little man featured in the centre of a triangle or within a closed design – it will be possible to analyse the corporal topology from both the inside and the outside.

The prevalence of converse images indicates a structuring of the subject with regard to the principle of pleasure: the subject is included in the relation with the other and draws his pleasure from it.

This observation can indicate as much a case of massive regression, of objective passivity, as a type of merging relation or temperament centring on the joy he experiences from his relationship with the world around him.

The successive study of three drawings and their differences is going to enable such a perception to be better tuned. The white sheet of paper will be treated to a number of possible concepts and the study of the objectified fantasies can vary according to what one sees from one design to another.

Some examples of the types of design that can be created, along with explanations of their composition in relation to the final interpretation, appear below.

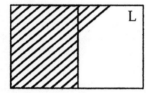 

Position of the design or little man in the space

The left part (L) indicates attachment to one's father, to the past, the fear of authority, a deeply rooted sense of values and belief in the family and also the feeling of guilt.

The right part (R) indicates someone turned towards the future, open to new ideas, ambitious, quick to learn, straining to achieve goals and extrovert.

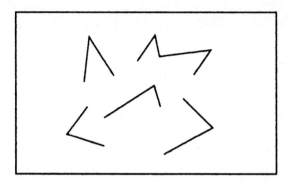

Predominance of angles

The predominance of angles, forming thorns or stars, indicates aggression, defiance, rebellion, impulsiveness, violence, a dare-devil or someone of a determined nature and looking for conflict.

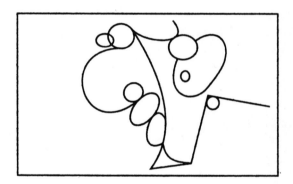

Predominance of rounded shapes

Where there is a majority of circular shapes – in loops, twirls or crowns – or soft, fluid themes without stress and not all tangled up, this indicates a tendency towards resignation, passivity, weakness or superficiality, carelessness, improvisation or lack of character.

The fluidity of the rounded shapes expresses easiness and banality and can also be a sign of the subject's lack of constructive sense or even delusion.

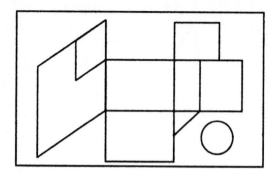

Predominance of squares

The 'squared' design is generally that of a solid individual, realistic, down-to-earth, endowed with a good provincial sense which can sometimes be heavy and devoid of imagination but is in any case constructive. The subject is a worker, methodical, sometimes slow and humourless, but most of the time efficient.

Predominance of circles

A majority of circles containing clean and well-defined lines translates the sentiment of the shape, an intuitive type, with flexibility in relationships, searching for harmony and with a sense of diplomacy.

More than 80 per cent of circular shapes in the drawing indicates a lack of constructive sense. Here the circle is taken by the subject as an empty form, without contents or significance.

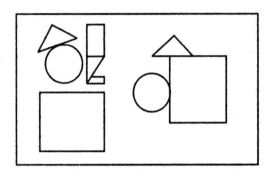

If the design is divided into several separate images

Here one is faced with a process of isolation which indicates a logical mind, aware of the symmetry of the drawings, secretive and perhaps deceitful, a flexible individual who avoids conflicts, sensitive and at the same time methodical, possessing an aptitude for reasoning and analysis.

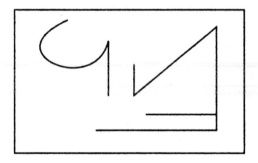

Predominance of open shapes

The predominance of open shapes indicates a liability towards instinct, a lack of the sense of limit or inhibition and with a gift for expression. The possibility of emotional or nervous release and the inability for self-control can correspond as much to a primary and aggressive character as to one with a temperament for tragedy.

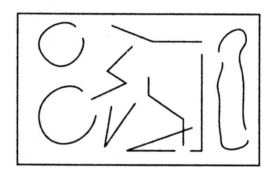

Broken lines

Broken lines reveal indetermination or indecision, emotional fragility or nervousness, lack of perseverance, a multitude of aims without any precise objective, instability.

The positive aspect of this meddlesome side is that the subject is a curious individual, an inventor or nomad, capable of creating different goals and multiple social solutions.

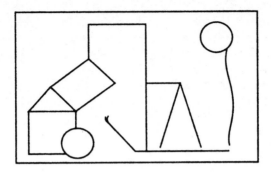

The harmonic design

This type of design, which tends generally to remain con-
stant from one drawing to another, indicates a balanced
mind, which 'composes' the picture and enriches it with
new possibilities, the capacity to integrate each of the new
elements so that they all have a significance, the active confrontation with reality and the harmonising of instincts. The
subjects of this type normally opt for an activity associated
with sensitivity.

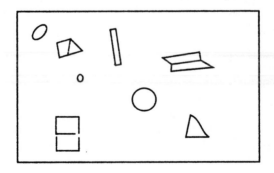

Design structured by scattered elements

The absence of any reference to a group indicates a lack of concentration, liaison or support, the tendency to give way, to refuse confrontation with reality, flight or passivity.

This looseness of ideas can be accompanied by a scrupulousness and concern for detail that can lead the subject to achieve tasks which require extreme attention and a particular finish.

Design carrying spaces inside the shapes

The elements of an unfinished design or one with some inner spaces reveal traumatism, a difficulty to learn, psychic mayhem or idea problems. Such a drawing can indicate as much a weakness of desire as a lack of co-ordination.

THE WORDS TEST

The instructions are as follows:

Each candidate must read carefully (at least twice) the list of words proposed. Afterwards each will be asked to choose a certain number and to separate them out into the following categories:

1. FAMILY	(5 words)
2. MONEY	(5 words)
3. BUSINESS	(5 words)

4. AUTHORITY   (5 words)
5. WORK   (5 words)
6. SUCCESS   (5 words)
7. FAILURE   (5 words)
8. MORALS   (5 words)

In total, the sheet of paper will have to contain 45 words – that is, five words for each category: family, business, work, success, etc. No word can be used twice – either in the same or a different category. In other words, the candidate can only use each word once. Half-an-hour is the time allowed for this test.

ILLNESS	UNDERSTANDING	NIGHTMARE
HEAT	SADNESS	SENSIBILITY
NAUSEA	COLD	FRAGILITY
RESPONSIBILITY	MIGRAINE	POVERTY
DISCONTENT	COMBATIVENESS	INSOMNIA
WEALTH	MISTRUST	FRIENDSHIP
FATIGUE	ATTRACTION	JUDGEMENT
TRUST	NERVOUSNESS	REPULSION
PUNISHMENT	SLEEP	DRUNKENNESS
HABIT	TROUBLE	CALM
NOISE	SILENCE	MISFORTUNE
STRENGTH	IRRITATION	AUTHORITY
REPROACH	PLEASURE	AGGRESSION
REVOLT	CRITICISM	EVIDENCE
ANGER	INTEREST	PAIN
JOY	HATE	GAIN
BOREDOM	FACILITY	BLUSH
LOSS	FEAR	TRUTH
PALENESS	FIDELITY	RESIGNATION
RECIPROCITY	TREMORS	DUTY
SOLITUDE	DYNAMISM	BURN
LOVE	LIE	EFFICIENCY
CRAMP	BENEFIT	ABANDON
FOOD	ANXIETY	DESIRE
THEFT	CURE	STRESS
OBSTINACY	WEAKNESS	ESTEEM
OBSESSION	ECONOMY	WORRY
RECOGNITION	IMPULSE	EXPENDITURE
DOUBT	SINCERITY	ANGUISH

LUXURY	SUFFERING	AFFECTION
DISTRACTION	SECURITY	OBSTACLE
CO-OPERATION	TEARS	AUTONOMY
SEVERITY	PASSIVITY	INHIBITION
ACCOMPLISHMENT	INJUSTICE	PROFITABILITY
DUMBNESS	GOAL	TREACHERY
TRANQUILLITY	COMPLICITY	EMOTION

Interpretation

This relatively simple test – both to use and to interpret – aims to reveal certain personality tendencies, without going particularly deeply into the principles.

There are four scales which apply here, according to the responses given: Scale 1 and Scale 2 (positive or negative connotations), the Stress Scale and the Neutral Scale.

To interpret the replies, one just has to transfer each of the words used to its scale of reference and to add up the number of words under each scale to determine the over-riding and underlying tendencies.

The rest of the interpretation depends on the judgement of the psychologist, according to one's own personality and the demands of the job. One can, for example, be looking for a co-operative, understanding and quiet individual or, on the other hand, someone who is particularly combative, dynamic and concerned about profitability.

It is therefore a question of adjusting the final interpretation of the results depending on the characteristics and profile of the job or the company.

The list of words corresponding to each scale appears below, followed by explanations relating to the interpretation of the different scales.

Scale 1 (positive connotations)

UNDERSTANDING	SENSIBILITY	RESPONSIBILITY
COMBATIVENESS	FRIENDSHIP	TRUST
SLEEP	CALM	EMOTION
STRENGTH	PLEASURE	JOY
FACILITY	TRUTH	RECIPROCITY
DYNAMISM	EFFICIENCY	FOOD

CURE	ESTEEM	RECOGNITION
SINCERITY	AFFECTION	CO-OPERATION
PROFITABILITY	TRANQUILLITY	COMPLICITY

Scale 2 (negative connotations)

ILLNESS	SADNESS	FRAGILITY
DISCONTENT	MISTRUST	JUDGEMENT
PUNISHMENT	TROUBLE	MISFORTUNE
REPROACH	CRITICISM	PAIN
BOREDOM	FEAR	RESIGNATION
SOLITUDE	ABANDON	LIE
THEFT	WEAKNESS	WORRY
DOUBT	SUFFERING	OBSTACLE
SEVERITY	INJUSTICE	TREACHERY

Stress Scale

NIGHTMARE	NAUSEA	MIGRAINE
INSOMNIA	FATIGUE	NERVOUSNESS
DRUNKENNESS	NOISE	IRRITATION
AGGRESSION	ANGER	HATE
BLUSH	PALENESS	TREMORS
BURN	CRAMP	ANXIETY
STRESS	OBSESSION	IMPULSE
ANGUISH	DISTRACTION	TEARS
INHIBITION	DUMBNESS	PASSIVITY

Neutral Scale

HEAT	COLD	POVERTY
WEALTH	ATTRACTION	REPULSION
HABIT	SILENCE	AUTHORITY
REVOLT	INTEREST	GAIN
LOSS	FIDELITY	DUTY
LOVE	BENEFIT	DESIRE
OBSTINACY	ECONOMY	EXPENDITURE
LUXURY	SECURITY	AUTONOMY
ACCOMPLISHMENT	GOAL	EVIDENCE

Stress Scale

The absence of any words included in the Stress Scale generally indicates that the candidate has deliberately avoided certain words with a negative connotation in order to appear in the best possible light. It is, for example, difficult to accept that words like migraine, fatigue, nervousness, irritation or stress are totally absent from the subject's pre-occupations, whether it is a question of work, success, failure or business.

Negative Scale

The total – or nearly total – absence of any words in the Negative Scale must be interpreted in the same way. There again, one would have trouble believing that the candidate could have such a rosy outlook on life, for example over questions of society or money. In such a case, one obviously takes the validity of the answers with a pinch of salt.

Where there is a majority of answers with a negative connotation, little comment is required. Clearly the candidate is not really on form. This can imply a transitory depressive state or neurotic tendencies, accentuated if reference to the Stress Scale is pertinent.

It is therefore necessary to interpret the results belonging to these two scales side by side in order to clarify the overall perception.

Positive & Neutral Scales

A majority of replies with positive connotations and of words belonging to the Neutral Scale indicate a good equilibrium, a harmonious integration of instincts and a capacity to produce and exchange ideas without too much difficulty.

Certain words such as MISFORTUNE, DISCONTENT, CRITICISM, WORRY, OBSTACLE or TROUBLE appearing in the WORK, MONEY and SUCCESS categories carry no special significance.

On the other hand words such as ILLNESS, LIE, THEFT, RESIGNATION, INJUSTICE, TREACHERY, DOUBT, PUNISHMENT, MISTRUST or FRAGILITY appearing in any of these categories risk being interpreted differently.

The same goes for the interpretation of the Stress Scale. Words like INSOMNIA, NOISE, ANXIETY, CRAMP, DISTRACTION, TEARS, FATIGUE or IRRITATION do not have any real effect on the analysis.

The assessment will be a lot more severe in other cases. Words such as AGGRESSION, ANGER, HATE, OBSES-

SION, INHIBITION, DRUNKENNESS, PASSIVITY, ANGUISH, REPULSION or REVOLT included in certain categories like SUCCESS, BUSINESS, WORK or SOCIETY will be interpreted in a negative way.

The categories

The same kind of analysis will be applied to categories such as FAMILY, MORALS or AUTHORITY. Certain words such as REPULSION, AGGRESSION, MISTRUST, REVOLT, ANGUISH or ANGER, for example, will create a bad impression there. Equally, words like BURN, ABANDON, NIGHTMARE, WEAKNESS, IMPULSE or NAUSEA added to those previously mentioned in the context of the other categories (see above).

The basic principles of the interpretation, as one can see, are thus relatively simple and the psychologist's work will essentially consist of linking certain words to the type of work involved.

If this involves placing a candidate in a position where there is regular contact with the general public, words like TRANQUILLITY, CALM and COMBATIVENESS (Positive Scale) or DUMBNESS, INHIBITION, SILENCE and REVOLT (Negative or Neutral Scale) will be adversely interpreted.

On the other hand, if the job is for a forester, the word SOLITUDE figuring in the WORK category will be considered as a positive indication. The same would apply in the case of a job involving mobility and travel. Words like AUTONOMY under the WORK category or TROUBLE under the FAMILY category will be interpreted favourably.

Word such as COLD, PROFITABILITY, JUDGEMENT and STRESS can also be judged favourable in the case of certain types of work. On the other hand, if it involves a communication job, the candidate runs a serious risk of being eliminated.

These different examples show the way in which this test is analysed.

Subsidiary replies

Certain categories, for example MORALS, AUTHORITY or FAILURE, could be analysed more closely depending on the circumstances. It is up to the candidate to avoid major pitfalls. It speaks for itself that words like NIGHTMARE, PUNISHMENT or MISTRUST will not go down well when placed in the WORK category. The same goes for REPULSION or NAUSEA.

Words like AGGRESSION or THEFT figuring in the MONEY category or BOREDOM, TROUBLE or COMPLICITY in the MORALS category will equally not be regarded very favourably. Examiners rarely have a sense of humour and this kind of reply is always penalised.

Therefore WORK must be a JOY, SOCIETY an ACCOMPLISHMENT, AUTHORITY a RESPONSIBILITY, MORALS an EVIDENCE, SUCCESS a GOAL, FAMILY a DUTY and so on.

So it is advisable to make a little effort and not to consider the sitting of a test as an excuse for self-expression (whatever the candidate feels about the range of subjects) or an amusement without consequence. The best advice is to adopt a suitable strategy and gear one's replies to the type of vacancy on offer. In this respect, any attempt to woo the examiner by means of humour or fantasy will be in vain.

The ideal approach will be one of reflexion and guile, the ability to adapt to the circumstances and the demands of the post – and, above all, to use one's common-sense.

In order to achieve that, as has already been made clear, one must avoid replies that characterise certain tendencies – neurosis or inadaptability, for example – or those that influence the examiner in a negative sense. Equally one should not opt for the 'harmless' or possibly obvious response 'like everyone else'. One is free to admit that one does occasionally get bored or suffers from migraines and that certain colleagues do get on one's nerves.

The other aspect of this type of test, as has already been mentioned, concerns a careful and thorough analysis of the work involved. This can only be done job by job and will, of course, depend in each case on the circumstances.

It is down to each candidate to be well-informed and, if possible, to adapt as required.

THE 18 IMAGES TEST

This last test is a little misleading. It could be said to belong with the project tests, if it was not so close to the divinatory arts (astrology, palmistry, etc) used today by certain recruitment bureaux.

The instructions are as follows:

The candidate is presented the 18 images illustrated overleaf one after the other and is asked to choose twelve and put them in the following four categories (three in each):

1. What represents the candidate, what he likes (3 images to choose).
2. What does not represent the candidate, his opposite, what he does not like (3 images to choose).
3. What the candidate attaches the most importance to in life (3 images to choose).
4. What the candidate ignores, what he rejects as being of least importance (3 images to choose).

The remaining images which the candidate does not select (there will be six) are put to one side and play no part in the final interpretation. Roughly five minutes is allocated for this test.

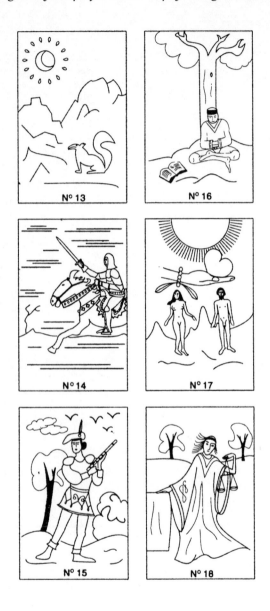

Nº 13

Nº 16

Nº 14

Nº 17

Nº 15

Nº 18

Interpretation

Here are the meanings attributed to each of the 18 images, which will have to be adapted according to the category in which the candidate places them.

Image No 1 – Mountain, day & sun
This first image evokes space, the ideal of purity and emptiness, silence, elevation and hope (represented by the star).

The absence of a person must be noted here if the image is placed in **Category 2 or 4**. Interiority, silence and solitude within himself are feared by the candidate or excluded from his world.

Image No 2 – Juggler
All the aspects of human ability, the play ideal and dexterity are represented in this image.

The juggler evokes the principle of action in both the material and mental world and the speed of liaison between ideas, words and things, two aspects of existence to which she dedicates all her skills.

Action, independence and creation are the three meanings taken in interpreting this image, according to which category the candidate places it in – that is to say, whether it is preferred, hated or ignored.

Image No 3 – Night storm
Solitude, night and the hostility of the natural elements which this drawing evokes often means it is placed in **Category 2 or 4**, what the candidate hates or rejects as of least importance in life.

The ill-omened aspect of this image (clouds, lightning, etc) evoke original chastisement, blame, ruin and above all sadness, the idea of solitude and obscurity.

The double notion of punishment and isolation in a hostile environment is involved in the interpretation of this picture.

Image No 4 – Throne
This picture represents the cube which epitomises one's own human make-up and the most accomplished form of matter. The idea of mastery, stability, organisation and order

summarises the whole meaning of this image.

Realisation in the material field, achievement, the possibility of culmination or, more simply, cementing an idea are the principle indications carried in this drawing.

Image No 5 – Sun

The solar star is here placed in the centre of the image, between two symmetrical structures, which evokes the notion of harmony and accord.

Balance, warmth, simplicity and clarity in one's feelings and ideas summarise the different meanings attributed to this picture.

Image No 6 – Traveller

The image of the man who turns his back and sets off towards an undetermined horizon evokes the notion of journeying, of change or of a voyage in search of new worlds, whether they exist in reality or just in the mind.

The idea of separation contained in that of journeying, of leaving to go elsewhere or pass on to other things, must also be interpreted according to the category in which the candidate has placed the image.

Image No 7 – Wounded heart

The meaning usually attached to this drawing, which is known to every culture, is retained here. It evokes love's pain and suffering, faithfulness, hope and sexual torment.

Image No 8 – Moon & water

This picture, which is very symbolic, represents creation and child-birth, the unconscious, dreams, psyche, the possibility of rebirth and all that is connected with the processes of growth and production.

The values of childhood, of apparent passivity and of invisible evolution are attached to these three symbols (moon, darkness and water), as well as the idea of evolution and biological rhythms.

Image No 9 – Knight

Conquest, self-assertion and the knight's desire to overcome make this a classic model. Placed in **Category 2 or 4**, it reverses the values and indicates passivity, lack of self-confidence and a general or transitory pessimism on the part of the candidate.

Image No 10 – Captive
The themes of constraint, imprisonment and forced immobilisation contained in this picture mean that it is often placed in **Category 2 or 4**, when it is not put in the discarded pile of images.

When included in **Category 1 or 3**, it evokes possible traumatism, obsession or a momentarily difficult situation in life for the candidate and implies intolerable constraints.

Image No 11 – Stars
This picture representing stars is one of hope and brightness. It symbolises nature, which delivers its secrets through love, regeneration and comfort within harmonious and independent surroundings.

The idea of inspiration, teaching and new activities is the general meaning given to this image, which is also one of vocation.

Image No 12 – Wreath
The eagle and the plaited wreath which surrounds it are symbols that speak enough for themselves and need no real explanation. This image represents honour, crowning, achievement and strength.

Placed in **Category 2 or 4**, it can signal disappointment and indicate on the part of the candidate a certain bitterness or contempt of any consideration or social success.

Image No 13 – Dog & moon
Imagination, dreams, sleep, reflexion and illusion – all of which this picture conjures up – are the symbolic values traditionally attached to this classic representation.

The moving aspect of the quickest of the heavenly bodies, from different quarters, linked with the to and fro action of the ocean, gives this image all the feminine characteristics. It is therefore with this meaning that the picture is to be interpreted, regardless of the category in which it is placed – positive or negative.

Image No 14 – Knight & storm
The aspect of torment in this drawing is enough to distinguish it from the conquering knight of **Image No 9**. Here the elements work against conquest and progress. The knight must confront the storm and it is the idea of obstacles and difficulty which must be foremost in the interpretation.

The values attached to the image of the knight are however retained (see **Image No 9**) and are part of the overall interpretation.

Image No 15 – Minstrel
The arts (all of them), freedom and facility which are evoked in this image make it one of inspiration and artistic expression.

These two ideas sum up the whole picture, whatever the category in which the candidate places it.

Image No 16 – Pastor
The pastoral reader shown here perhaps represents Virgil or Homer. In any event, it evokes the acquisition of knowledge in the calm and silence of rustic countryside, the necessary solitude for study and the slow progression of ideas.

Image No 17 – Harmony
This image, which is often preferred to others, evokes the idea of a couple, alliance and fullness, but also that of conscience and the radiation of speech and culture as represented by the sun.

All its significance is epitomised by language, activity and the human couple. It embodies the values of clarity and harmony, refraction of the spirit in matter and conquest through communication.

Image No 18 – Scales
This final image symbolises justice and all that goes with it. Equity, merit, rigour, incorruptibility and the idea of fair retribution or a new equilibrium are the principle notions used in interpreting this picture, according to where the candidate has placed it.

A few final words...
This last 'test', which falls midway between project tech-niques and the divinatory arts, is likely to strike the candidate as not being particularly strenuous or exacting. And rightly so.

This type of test or method can no more be considered a means of selection than palmistry or astrology.

It is therefore up to the reader, when interpreting these 18 images, to put himself in the position of poet or fortune-teller, to let his imagination take over and to regard this 'test' as a game... or a dream.

CONCLUSION

The objective throughout this book has been to present the principles of the construction of those tests that measure professional aptitude, intelligence, 'personality', character or temperament similar to those used by recruitment agencies.

The presentation of various exercises and questionnaires therefore seemed the best way of enlightening those who run a serious risk of having to subject themselves to this type of examination in the context of a candidate's selection.

The paradoxical (and psychological) effect of the **Practical Tests** should bear this out. Those readers who have scored badly in these tests (quite probably the majority of you!) will be able to reassure themselves in discovering that the conclusions correspond neither to reality nor their actual competence.

One can clearly be forgiven for regarding as rather curious the fact that a part of the population can be subjected to professional selection exams without knowing, at least in general terms, of what this kind of instrument consists and what it aims to determine.

The hazardous evaluation of 'intelligence'
It is important to underline, in the most concrete way possible, how often these methods of recruitment are subject to error, particularly in the case of selection by 'intelligence'. The indications furnished by intelligence tests have often only little relevance to the results obtained by the subjects examined on their own studies or in the course of their profession.

As far as evaluating intelligence or skills, judging individual's activities, knowing how people function mentally or emotionally, detecting eventual conflicts or finding out social attitudes or one's conception of the world or a business or society are concerned, the conclusions that can be drawn remain very hazardous ones and the replies given by each candidate should be the subject of considerable caution.

The analysis of a CV, diplomas or professional experience, an understanding of the demands of the job and an interview with the candidate provide the most valuable information. Certainly, these elements are less exhaustive than those that are supposed to be obtained through tests. But in the majority of cases they are more exact – and that can often prove more useful.

Being familiar with tests

After having compared actual results with the predictions of aptitude tests, the more intelligent are perhaps going to realise that selection by means of such tests in no way enables one to foresee success or failure in any given career.

That is not the question. It is simply a case of the reader preparing himself for the best – and at the same time worst – possible situation and knowing what risks he is running if one day he finds himself subjected to this type of test.

The aim of this book will have been achieved if the future candidate is able to familiarise himself with this kind of examination, to know the principles (often very simple) and not to be too surprised, when the time comes, by what he is being asked to do.

And, finally, that he also finds in it some gentle encouragement to succeed.